cocker spa

understanding and caring for your breed

Written by
Jane Simmonds

cocker spaniel

understanding and
caring for your breed

Written by
Jane Simmonds

Pet Book Publishing Company

Bishton Farm, Bishton Lane, Chepstow, NP16 7LG, United Kingdom.
881 Harmony Road, Unit A, Eatonton, GA31024 United States of America.

Printed and bound in China through Printworks International.

ISBN: 978-1-906305-68-0
ISBN: 1-906305-68-4

Acknowledgements

The publishers would like to
thank the following for help with
photography: Tracy Morgan
(www.animalphotographer.
co.uk), Jane Simmonds (Shenmore), Gill Moutrey (Sunzo), Andy Fisher
(Spinnchetti gundogs), Gareth Lawler (Roqfolly), and David Tomlinson
(page 14-15).

Text used in this edition was previously published in *Cocker Spaniel: An
Owner's Guide*.

Introducing the Cocker Spaniel

The Cocker Spaniel is the breed that has is all – good looks, intelligence, and personality plus. It is small wonder that he is one of the most popular of the sporting breeds.

The Cocker Spaniel was originally bred to flush out game for the gun, and this original role reflects his whole attitude to life. He is immensely busy, nose to the ground and tail wagging, intent on discovering every new sight and sound, and, most particularly, every scent he comes across.

He seems to have limitless energy and, come rain or shine, he is always ready to set off on an expedition, hoping that it will last all day!

However, there is another side to the Cocker. He is a most loving and affectionate dog, and he bonds closely with all members of his human family. He thrives on companionship, and likes to be involved in everything that is going on.

Physical characteristics

In many ways, the Cocker Spaniel is the perfect size; he is big enough to be a 'proper' dog, but small enough to fit into a family car, which means he can be included on most outings.

The Cocker has a most distinctive head, with a slightly domed skull, and long, pendulous ears framing his face. His dark eyes have a sweet expression which would melt the hardest of hearts. His body is balanced and in proportion, and although he is not a big dog, his movement is easy and ground covering.

The Cocker's coat is silky and close fitting, with a beautiful gleam. The feathering can be profuse on the ears and the tail, as well as on the legs and the underside of the body. This can look very glamorous when dogs are groomed for the show ring, but it is hard work to maintain, so many pet owners opt to have their Cockers trimmed.

The wide range of colors is a Cocker speciality, with a choice of solids, particolors and roans, so there is certain to be something to suit everyone.

We are fortunate that the Cocker is bred without exaggerations, and, with luck, he should live a healthy life, with few complications. In general, most Cockers live between 10 and 12 years, although many do better than this, surviving into their teens.

The adaptable cocker

The Cocker is one of the most versatile of breeds, which plays a big part in his popularity today. Whether you want a dog to show, work in the field or take part in sports such as agility, there is a Cocker Spaniel for you. However the Cocker's most popular role is undoubtedly as family companion. His cheerful nature, compact size, and good looks make him the ideal pet for many families.

The Cocker is an outstanding family companion.

He gets on well with children, perhaps being better suited to an older age group as he will provide plenty of entertainment.

He can learn to live with smaller children, but care needs to be taken as most Cockers, particularly when they are young, are full of exuberance and find it difficult to inhibit their behavior.

The Cocker thrives on exercise – and the more varied it is, the more he likes it. He is therefore ideally suited to an active family, or to owners who enjoy an outdoor lifestyle. He is relatively easy to care for, although his coat does need regular attention.

Although bred as a country dog, working as a shooting companion, the Cocker can adapt to city life, as long as his owners are prepared to give him the exercise he needs. In terms of accommodation, whether you live in an apartment or a mansion is immaterial for this conveniently sized breed, but access to a garden should be considered essential.

The Cocker is a sociable dog, and enjoys canine company. He will mix happily with most breeds, especially those that share his outlook on life.

Watch out, Cockers can be very collectable, and before you know it, you may find that one becomes two....

Trainability

The Cocker is quick-witted and intelligent, and needs to keep his mind occupied, otherwise he may invent his own entertainment, which may not be to your liking.

Just like any other dog, a Cocker needs careful socialization and training with an owner who understands how his mind works and how to get the best from him. If you can offer this, you will have a wonderful companion and a Cocker to be proud of!

This is a dog that needs leadership.

Tracing back
in time

The spaniel breeds have a long and colorful history, and although it is hard to separate fact from fiction, it seems that the first records date back to the 13th century.

It is often said that spaniels originated from Spain ('spaniel' being a corruption of the French word 'espagnol', meaning Spanish). This theory is based on sources such as the oldest English book on hunting, Master of Game (1406-1413) written by Edward Plantagenet, Duke of York, who wrote of spaniels that "their nature cometh from Spain". Although there is no real evidence to support this claim, it remains a popular theory today.

It is known that these early spaniels were sporting dogs, used in the hunting of wild fowl and falconry – helping to flush quarry into the hunting nets or towards trained birds of prey.

Dr Caius, a famed Elizabethan physician, describes these hunting spaniels in his Treatise of Englishe Dogges (translated from Latin in 1576), which was the earliest known attempt at a complete classification of dogs. He noted that the land spaniels were used for, "The Falcon, The Phesant, The Partridge and such like".

Cocking spaniels

Although spaniels had been used for centuries for sporting purposes, it was not until the 1800s that the Cocker or Cocking Spaniel emerged as a separate, distinct type.

The name derives from the use of small spaniels for woodcock shooting, which had become popular at the time. These 'cocking' spaniels could get into the thickest undergrowth and flush out the woodcock to the waiting guns.

One of the first mentions of cocking spaniels in literature can be found in The Sportsman's Cabinet written by William Taplin in 1803.

Taplin records that there were two types of spaniel at that time:

- The larger Springing Spaniel (forerunner of the modern Springer Spaniel), which was used on all kinds of game.

- The smaller Cocker or Cocking Spaniel, which was used for woodcock shooting "to which they are more particularly appropriated and by nature seem designed."

He describes the Cocker as having "a shorter, more compact form, a rounder head, shorter nose, ears long (and the longer, the more admired), the limbs short and strong, the coat more inclined to curl than the springers..."

Colors were liver and white, red, red and white, black and white, solid liver "and not infrequently black with tanned legs and muzzle." This confirms black and tan as one of the oldest Cocker colors.

In the later part of the 19th century, it seems that different strains of Cocker Spaniel had been developed in different parts of the country, such as the Welsh Cocker (later to become the Welsh Springer) and the Devon Cocker.

Stonehenge, the Victorian author, wrote in The Dog in Health and Disease (1859) that it was difficult to describe the Cocker in detail because there were so many regional variations, but generally he could be said to be "a light active spaniel of about 14lb weight on the average, sometimes reaching 20lb, with very elegant shapes, and a lively and spirited carriage."

Developing
the breed

The Victorian era saw rapid advances
in selective dog breeding and formal
record keeping with the founding of the
Kennel Club in 1873. Dog exhibiting
was also developed at this time with
the first organized dog show taking
place in 1859.

In the latter part of the 19th century, formal Field
Trials were also becoming recognized as a sport; the
first trials specifically for spaniels were held in 1899
and won by a Cocker named Stylish Pride.

In early Kennel Club stud books, there was no
separate classification of the Cocker Spaniel, despite
the breed's long history. Instead Field Spaniels
were divided into "Over 25lb" and "Under 25lb" with
Cockers included in this latter category.

This did not change until 1893 when the Kennel Club
finally recognized the Cocker Spaniel as a separate

breed but still retained the weight limit of 25lb. Up to this time, it was not unusual for Cockers and Field Spaniels to be born in the same litter and be entered in different classes at shows, depending on how much they weighed.

Cocker enthusiasts were deeply opposed to the arbitrary weight limit of 25lb being imposed by the Kennel Club, arguing that type was far more important than weight. Not surprisingly, the breed made little progress during this time with the Field Spaniel being by far the more popular breed – a situation that is reversed today. Eventually the Kennel Club removed the weight limit in 1901.

A year later, the Cocker Spaniel Club was formed and a Breed Standard was drawn up by a committee which was composed mainly of shooting men. Although the Standard has been amended slightly over subsequent decades, it remains the same, in essence, today as it was when it was first produced.

Traveling to the USA

It is believed that the first spaniel travelled to the USA on the Mayflower in 1620, but it was not until 1878 that the first Cocker Spaniel was imported from England and registered with the American Kennel Club. Three years later, a breed club was established. But it was the birth of Obo II that put the breed on the map.

In the UK, a Cocker called Ch. Obo, born in 1879, had proved to be a successful show dog and a highly influential sire. Indeed, he is regarded as the foundation of the Cocker Spaniel breed.

An American Cocker Spaniel breeder, Mr Pitcher tried to buy Ch. Obo from his British owner, James Farrow, but Farrow was adamant that his dog was not for sale. However, after much persuasion, he agreed on a compromise. He agreed to part with a Cocker bitch called Chloe II, a successful show dog in her own right, who was in whelp to Ch. Obo. Chloe was shipped to the USA, and Ch. Obo II became the star member of the resulting litter, and the foundation of the breed in its new home.

The early 20th century Cocker

From the early 1900s, the Cocker Spaniel went from strength to strength on both sides of the Atlantic. They were valued working in the field – those in the USA were used for retrieving quail – and were also making their mark in the show ring.

During this time, the breed evolved in type quite markedly.

When Ch. Obo was in his heyday, Cockers were quite different in size and proportion to today's Cocker, as can be demonstrated by Obo's vital statistics. He weighed 22lb, was only 10 inches (25cm) high, and measured 29 inches (33cm) from nose to tail, so we can see that he was quite a small dog, long in body and quite low to the ground. Colors most often seen at this time were solid liver, liver and tan, solid black, black and tan.

The fashion for long, low dogs continued for some time, but eventually a taller, more symmetrical Cocker evolved during the first part of the 20th century. This was largely due to the influence of the early Cocker pioneers, such as Mr C.A. Phillips (Rivington), R. De Courcy Peele (Bowdler) and Mr Richard Lloyd, who used outcrosses to Field Spaniels, Springer Spaniels and English Setters to increase size.

More colors also began to be seen, including blue roan and solid red – the latter due to judicious imports from North America. Mention must also be made of H.S. Lloyd, who inherited his father's (Richard Lloyd) kennel in 1906 and founded the world famous Of Ware line of Cockers, which continues today in the ownership of his daughter, Jennifer Lloyd-Carey. The Of Ware dogs had an enormous influence on the breed's development, and Mr Lloyd's record of six Best in Show wins at Crufts with three different Cockers is unlikely ever to be surpassed.

What should a Cocker Spaniel look like?

Like every pedigree breed, the Cocker Spaniel has a Breed Standard which is a written blueprint describing the most desirable features in terms of temperament and physical appearance.

Dogs entered at shows are judged against the Standard, but it is important to stress that Breed Standards do not just describe the perfect show dog. The Cocker Standard was originally drawn up by men who worked their dogs, and while there have been some minor amendments, the Standard still retains the original emphasis on a dog that is fit for his original function as a sporting dog.

Dog Expert | 29

General appearance

The Cocker is a compact, sturdy dog, free from exaggerations. He is sometimes described as being "cobby", using equine terminology for a short-backed, stocky, little horse. He is well balanced, measuring about the same from the top of the shoulder blades (the withers) to the floor as from the same point to the base of his tail. However, in practice many modern show dogs are slightly shorter in the body than the Standard describes.

Characteristics

The Cocker has a merry nature with a constantly wagging tail. He has a busy, bustling movement, particularly when following a scent, and will happily force his way through the thickest cover. Although the bustling is perhaps more obvious in a working dog, even the owner of a pet Cocker will recognise this description as they watch their dog eagerly following his nose into the nearest available undergrowth!

Temperament

The Cocker is happy and extrovert – a subdued, timid personality is definitely alien for the breed. He has a kind, gentle temperament and is very affectionate, often greeting complete strangers as if they were long-lost friends. He expects his affection to be

Points of anatomy

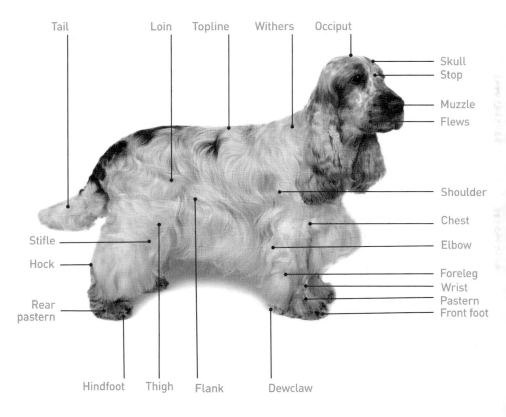

Tail

Loin

Topline

Withers

Occiput

Skull

Stop

Muzzle

Flews

Shoulder

Chest

Stifle

Elbow

Hock

Foreleg

Wrist

Rear
pastern

Pastern

Front foot

Hindfoot

Thigh

Flank

Dewclaw

reciprocated by all he meets and can be confused when this is not always forthcoming! He is also energetic and enthusiastic. "Life is for living" could be his motto, as he likes to be on the go, wanting to get involved in everything his family is doing.

Head and skull

The Cocker has a balanced head with the skull about the same length as the foreface (the stop is the indentation between the eyes).

The muzzle needs to be square not snipey (weak and pointed) to give sufficient strength to the lower jaw.

The skull is slightly domed but not in an exaggerated way; round, apple heads are not desirable. The head should not be too broad, although wide, white markings on the head of a particolored dog can give the optical illusion of an over-broad skull when this is not actually the case.

Nose

The Cocker needs a good-sized nose with wide, open nostrils to help him perform his function as a working dog, sniffing out fallen game.

Eyes

The eyes should be full and slightly oval in shape, not too large or prominent in any way. Large, prominent

Facing page: A sound temperament is a hallmark of the breed.

eyes would be more prone to injury in the field. The rims should be tight, because loose bottom lids would hinder a working dog, making the eyes more susceptible to infection or injury.

Eyes should be dark brown or brown, except for liver-colored dogs (solids and particolors) where a lighter shade of brown (hazel) is permitted. This is because the liver color gene has a fading effect on eye color, making it impossible for dark-brown eyes to be produced – although the greeny/yellow eyes seen on some liver dogs are not desirable.

A Cocker can use his eyes to look sad and doleful on occasion (as any owner knows), but, in general, the Cocker has a sweet, gentle expression and his eyes reflect his intelligence and his cheerful, good nature.

Ears

The Cocker is well known for his long, pendulous ears, which are set on level with the eyes. The ear flaps (leathers) should extend to the tip of the nose.

Cocker ears, particularly on show dogs, can look longer than they are, as the hair on a mature dog's ear can grow inches longer than the length of the actual leathers. This is why a pet Cocker whose hair has been clipped short can look as if he has much shorter ears than a dog in full show coat.

Facing page: The long, pendulous ears frame the face.

Neck

The neck should be moderate in length and muscular. A Cocker needs to have strong neck muscles to be able to lift and carry game, but the neck must not be too long or too short. Too long a neck makes the dog look unbalanced and exaggerated; too short a neck is usually associated with poor shoulder angulation and makes the dog look very 'stuffy'.

The neck should join the body smoothly with no lumps and bumps where it meets the shoulders, and there should be no excess loose skin on the throat.

Mouth

As a gundog breed, expected to be able to carry quite heavy game for some distance without damage, it is important for a Cocker to have good, strong jaws and the correct scissor bite, with the teeth on the upper jaw closely overlapping the teeth on the lower jaw. Show judges often place great importance on correct bites, because a faulty bite is very difficult to breed out and would also prevent the dog from carrying out his original working function.

Forequarters

The dog's shoulder assembly is made up of the shoulder blade and the upper arm. These bones should be "well laid back", meaning they slope backwards and ideally form close to a right angle where they meet. Well-laid-back shoulders give a good reach of neck, sufficient width to the body, and the long, economical stride essential for a sporting dog with the stamina to work all day.

A Cocker also needs to have strong, straight, well-boned legs. As a small breed originally intended to work through thick cover (undergrowth), long legs are not required. But the legs should not be too short and stumpy, as this would affect the dog's ability to work, as well as giving an unbalanced appearance.

The body is short,
square and compact.

Body

The Cocker has a short, square body with well-rounded ribs, giving plenty of room for the heart and lungs. The depth of body is about the same as the length of leg. The rib cage is deep and should go right down to the elbow and extend as far back as the loin. The muscular area between the end of the ribs and the hindquarters (the couplings) needs to be short and strong, as this area helps power the hindquarters.

The topline (meaning the line of the back) should be firm and straight, only starting to slope gently from the end of the loin down to where the tail starts, contributing to the rounded rump the Cocker is known for.

Hindquarters

A Cocker should have broad, well-muscled thighs and a well-bent stifle to give him the strength and power needed to do his job of work, thrusting under thick cover etc. A well-bent stifle is produced when the upper and lower thigh bones are a good length and are laid back at a sufficient angle where they meet at the stifle joint. Good angulation here produces a hock joint that is relatively low to the ground, allowing the dog to drive well from behind.

Feet

A Cocker needs round, well-cushioned, tight feet to protect him when he is working; thin, flat feet with spreading toes are not desirable, as they are more prone to injury and will offer little in the way of cushioning to support the dog's body on a long day in the field.

Tail

The Cocker is famous for his ever-wagging tail and is known worldwide as the 'merry Cocker'.

Originally, the Cocker was traditionally a docked breed, with a portion of the tail removed after birth in order to prevent tail injuries when working. However, tail docking is now banned in the UK, and most parts of Europe, and is only permitted where there is evidence that the dog is intended for working. In the USA, tail docking is still permitted, regardless of whether the dog is to be worked.

The tail is set on just below the level of the back, but not too low, and is carried level with the back. Sometimes when excited, the tail is carried higher,

We are now accustomed to seeing Cockers with tails.

particularly noticeable in a male. The undocked tail is well feathered, slightly curved, and ideally should not extend beyond the dog's hock joint (an overlong tail can give an unbalanced appearance).

Gait/movement

The Cocker is a sound, free-moving dog, with the front and back legs moving parallel in a straight line, turning neither in nor out. As mentioned before, good angulation in the forehand (shoulder) and hindquarters means he can use long strides to cover the ground well, which is so important in a working dog.

Coat

A Cocker should have a close-fitting, flat, silky coat on his body with feathering on his legs and underneath his body. The feathering not only looks attractive but helps to protect the body from injury when working. The coat should not be "too profuse", as a very long, thick coat would get caught up in the undergrowth and be a positive hindrance to a working dog.

Many modern show Cockers do grow very thick coats with long feathering, which looks very glamorous when presented correctly but would be quite impracticable for a working dog. Dogs bred from working lines tend to have much sparser coats for this reason.

Color

Cocker spaniels come in a variety of colors, which include:

Solid colors: Black; red; golden; liver (chocolate); black and tan; liver and tan.

Particolors: Black and white; orange and white; liver and white; lemon and white. "And whites" means the background color of the coat is pure white with no roaning. These colors may or may not have ticking (small flecks of color on the white background), which is referred to as "and white ticked" e.g. black and white ticked.

Tricolors: Black, white and tan; liver, white and tan.

Roans: Intermixed white and colored hairs of any color. In Cockers this may be blue roan; orange roan; lemon roan; liver roan; blue roan and tan; liver roan and tan.

In the UK Breed Standard there is a list of accepted colors. In the US types of color are defined (e.g. solid colors, particolors), and a description of tan points (where they should appear, and to what extent).

The Cocker probably has more coat color variations than any other breed, although some colors are more commonly seen than others.

In recent years, the sable coloring has become more popular. Sable refers to a basically black (or liver dog) where tan markings have spread extensively underneath the coat, mixing with the black (or liver) hairs. Sable particolors are also possible. Sable is somewhat controversial; it has probably existed for many years, but it is now considered undesirable under the UK Breed Standard as revised in 2012, although it remains acceptable in the US.

Size

There is a difference in size in the height and weight stipulations for the Cocker in the USA and the Cocker in the UK.

The Kennel Club (KC) asks for males to be approximately 39-41cm (15^1/$_2$ -16in), and for bitches to be approximately 38-39cm (15-15^1/$_2$in). Weight is approximately: 13 to 14.5kg (28-32lb). The American Kennel Club (AKC) allows dogs to be a full inch (2.5cm) taller, and 2lb (0.9kg) heavier.

Both Standards agree that a male should be a little bigger and heavier than a female, but note that the weights and heights given are approximate only (the lessons have been learned from the old days when Cockers were given an arbitrary weight limit that had to be complied with). The Cocker is essentially a 'big dog in a small package', but his weight should come

Facing page. Gold (top left), Black, Blue roan, Orange and white, Black and tan, Tricolor.

from his sturdy bone and muscular body – he should never be fat or flabby.

Summing up

The Cocker Spaniel has come a long way since the breed was first developed as a purely working dog in the 19th century. Nowadays, this is a truly versatile breed with worldwide popularity as a family pet and show dog. But the Cocker's sporting roots have not been forgotten. Working Cockers have become increasingly popular in recent years and have a dedicated following, whether this be for the demands of competitive Field Trials or as weekend shooting companions.

Although Cockers have certainly changed over the years, most noticeably the development into two distinct strains, some things remain the same. Whether show or working-type, a Cocker is still the same small, sturdy dog with a big personality, always ready to throw himself enthusiastically into everything life has to offer!

What do you want from your Cocker?

Before you make any definite arrangements to buy a Cocker puppy, or adopt an older dog, it is a good idea to sit down and think about all the pros and cons, since owning a dog is a lifetime commitment and should never be taken lightly.

The first thing to consider is whether a Cocker really is suitable for your family's lifestyle. Most people fall for the Cocker because of his attractive looks, his famous "merry" temperament and his compact size – being not too big but not too small either – but some fail to realize that this is no lap dog!

A Cocker Spaniel is a busy, energetic dog, and likes to be involved in everything that is going on. He thrives in a family situation, and as long as interactions are supervised and mutual respect established, he will be a lively and playful companion for children.

This is a dog that loves to use his nose, and go for long rambles, so if you are looking for an active dog that is always ready to get up and go, you will not be disappointed.

Show or working?

It is important to understand the differences between the two distinct Cocker strains – show-type and working – so that you can make the right choice for your family and lifestyle. Show-type dogs will be instantly recognizable to most people, having the typical domed head, long ears and glamorous coat with abundant feathering.

As the name suggests, this is the type of Cocker seen at shows where dogs are judged against the Breed Standard. However, it is important to realize that many commercial breeders produce show-type Cockers. But 'show-type' does not mean that the breeder shows their dogs, or that their puppies will be show quality; it simply means that they resemble this general type to a greater or lesser degree.

Show-type dogs have been popular as family pets for many years, although their long feathering means that regular grooming and trimming are needed to keep the coat neat and tidy. Would-be owners also need to realize that just because a Cocker comes from show lines does not mean he has lost all the characteristics of a working gundog. Many show-type dogs like to pick up and carry items around. They will also use their noses to hunt through undergrowth like their working ancestors, although perhaps without the speed of today's purpose-bred Working Cockers.

Although few show-type Cockers today do the job that they were originally bred for, there are still a handful of dedicated owners who work their show dogs to demonstrate that they have not lost their working abilities.

Working Cockers have become increasingly popular in recent years and are no longer confined to working homes as once was the case. Dogs are bred primarily for their working ability with less importance placed on conformation to the official Breed Standard. This means that a Working Cocker can look somewhat different to his show-type cousin.

His skull is usually flatter and broader, without the slight dome of a show dog. His ears are shorter and his body often appears longer and leggier than a show dog. There is quite a variation in size from very large to quite small, so it is not possible to say that Working Cockers are always bigger or smaller than show-type dogs.

A working-type dog usually carries far less coat than a show dog, although there is, again, some variation, as some have thicker coats than others. This lack of coat means that a Working Cocker can appeal to owners who do not want to do much grooming, but there needs to be a clear understanding that there is a lot more to a Working Cocker than a short coat!

As he was bred to work, he will usually have the kind of speed and stamina to enable him to work in the field all day. While it is unfair to generalize too much, it is true to say that many Working Cockers are far more energetic than show-type Cockers; some can be on the go all day and still be up for more at the end of it!

A Cocker bred from working lines needs a more active lifestyle.

What does your Cocker want from you?

The Cocker Spaniel has a happy outlook on life and his demands are few. However, like all animals, he has his own special needs, and you need to take these on board in order to provide a suitable home.

The Cocker Spaniel has a loving and affectionate nature and he thrives on human companionship. With the correct training, he is not clingy and will accept times when he is on his own. But if you have a job that takes you away all day, this is not the breed for you. In fact, it could be that you should delay taking on any dog until your situation has changed.

There are care options, such as using the services of a dog sitter or a dog walker, but you need to check

credentials carefully to make sure the person you employ is trustworthy and capable of looking after your dog. You could also consider doggie day care, where dogs are looked after in someone's home, rather like a dog version of a nursery or kindergarten. Again, the success of these establishments is entirely dependent on the capabilities of the person or people running it.

Routine care

The Cocker is a relatively easy breed to care for, but you need to bear in mind that this is a long-haired breed that needs regular grooming and will shed hair (some more than others); he may not be the dog for you if you are exceptionally house proud. If you decide to keep your Cocker in a pet trim, you will need to budget for regular trips to the grooming parlor.

As well as grooming, your Cocker will need routine preventative health care, such as worming and flea treatments, and you will also need to set aside money, or take out insurance, for unexpected veterinary treatment.

Exercise

How much exercise a Cocker needs will depend on his age and also, to some extent, on whether he comes from show or working lines.

While young puppies (of both types) will only need short walks to begin with, a mature Cocker needs sufficient daily exercise to keep his mind and body healthy and happy. A Cocker that is not given enough exercise of the right kind can suffer from health problems, such as obesity, or behavioral issues brought about by boredom and frustration. A fit, healthy Cocker will enjoy as much exercise as you can give him, but this does not mean that he needs a 10-mile hike every day.

Many show-type dogs will be happy with two good 30 to 40-minute walks a day, plus access to the garden at regular intervals for play/training sessions. However, many Working Cockers will need considerably more exercise than this, perhaps up to three hours a day, depending on their age and fitness levels.

Mental stimulation

Cockers of both types need an opportunity to use their brains and natural instincts when being exercised. A Cocker needs some variety and will get bored going on the same walk every day. He will also need access to open areas where he can be let off the lead. Pavement walking on a lead does not offer a dog anywhere near as much exercise or mental stimulation as a walk that includes the opportunity for free running in a field or park.

Mental stimulation is especially important for Working Cockers; they need something to do to keep their minds and bodies occupied and they do best in a home where the owner provides the opportunity for activities such as canine agility or gundog training. They can and do make very good pets for the active family, but if you are a first-time dog owner with no experience of training an active working dog, a Working Cocker may not be the best choice for you.

Extra considerations

Now you have decided that a Cocker Spaniel is best suited to your family and your lifestyle you need to narrow your choice so you know exactly what you are looking for.

Male or female?

A male Cocker is usually slightly bigger and heavier than a female, but there is very little difference in temperament between the two sexes and both make equally good family pets.

Some say that bitches are easier to train and more affectionate. However, there is little evidence for this in Cockers and the theory is perhaps based on the bigger, guarding breeds. In reality, all Cockers have their own individual personalities, which are influenced less by gender and more by other factors such as genetics, socialization and training.

There are certain practical considerations that might influence your choice of a male or a female. Bitches come into season once or twice a year (depending on their cycle) from the age of six months onwards. During seasons, it is the owner's responsibility to keep their bitch safe from the attentions of entire male dogs. This means that exercise may have to be limited or confined to on-lead walks in areas where there are no other dogs around.

During and after seasons, a bitch may also be affected by behavioral changes, such as moodiness, due to the fluctuating hormone levels. There may also be a lapse in house-training, as in-season bitches tend to urinate more than normal.

Spaying a bitch will, of course, mean the end to her seasons and any of these issues, as well as having other health benefits. But note that some vets prefer not to spay until a bitch has had at least one season.

Many potential new owners are put off having a male because of fears that male dogs are difficult to let off the lead to exercise and will stray constantly, looking for the nearest bitch. In reality, both sexes will need persistent recall training, as their natural gundog instincts can make them 'selectively deaf' to the calls of their owner, especially when they are following a particularly interesting scent.

Facing page: Two puppies spell double the trouble.

Males can certainly be distracted by bitches, but generally only when there is a bitch in season in close proximity. A male can, of course, be neutered to reduce any excessive interest in the opposite sex, but neutering will not cure a dog with a poor recall – only training can do this.

More than one?

Some people make the mistake of thinking it is better to have two puppies at the same time because they will be able to keep each other company, especially if the owner works long hours and feels guilty about leaving a dog alone.

This is probably the worst reason to take on two pups, as two puppies left alone for long periods will inevitably entertain themselves in whatever way they can. This could mean barking, to the annoyance of your neighbors, or, even worse, they could decide to wreck your home. If you work long hours, it is not possible to have a dog or dogs unless you make suitable arrangements for their care.

There is another potential problem that could arise, particularly if both puppies are the same sex. Same-sex puppies may appear to get along very well at first, but it is not unusual for their relationship to deteriorate as they reach adolescence, resulting in squabbles and, in serious cases, major fights.

There is also the risk that two puppies bought at the same time can bond too closely with each other, especially if they are allowed to spend all their time together.

If you are a first-time owner without previous puppy training experience, it is better to start with one puppy that you can then devote all your attention to. You should never underestimate how demanding training just one puppy can be. You could then add to your canine family later, once your first Cocker is fully mature and well trained, which will not usually be before the age of 18 months.

Choosing a rescued dog

Can you give a rescued dog a second chance?

Although many people get their first Cocker as a puppy from a breeder, it should be remembered that there are many lovely dogs in rescue, often through no fault of their own.

Make sure the rescue organization you contact is reputable, as dog rescues are not currently regulated in any way. Reputable rescues will assess a dog as much as possible before rehoming and will also check out any potential new owners to make sure they can offer the right home for each particular dog. A good rescue will also offer back-up advice and support after a dog goes to a new home and will always take back a dog if this ever becomes necessary.

Sourcing
a puppy

If you see the mother with her puppies, you will get some idea of the temperament they are likely to inherit.

When you take on a Cocker Spaniel puppy, he will, hopefully, be your companion for the next dozen years or so. It is therefore worth spending time doing your homework so you find a healthy, well-reared pup that is typical of the breed.

Unfortunately, the popularity of the Cocker has meant that many puppies are bred by breeders who are only interested in making money at the expense of the health and welfare of their dogs. Often people looking for a Cocker puppy make the mistake of thinking that, as they want their dog to be "just a pet", it does not matter too much where their pup comes from.

Nothing could be further from the truth. If you are looking for a pet Cocker puppy, health and temperament should be very important priorities. No family wants a puppy with a poor temperament, or one which suffers from a preventable hereditary disease. Responsible breeders always breed for good temperament, and should also use the available health-testing schemes to ensure their pups grow up to be as healthy as possible.

Here are some pointers to bear in mind in your search for a breeder:

- Go to a specialist breeder, not one that constantly advertises large numbers of popular breeds for sale. A specialist breeder will have the knowledge and experience to discuss every aspect of the breed with potential buyers.

- Always see a litter of puppies with their mother and as many of the breeder's other dogs as possible. This will allow you to see for yourself that they have good temperaments and are happy to meet visitors. Never buy from a pet shop or dealer where puppies are bought in from other premises – usually puppy farms – to be sold to whoever has the cash to pay for them

- Expect to be asked as many questions by the breeder as you ask him/her. Good breeders will always want to know as much about potential buyers as possible to ensure that the home offered is right for one of their puppies.

- Always check whether the parents of a litter have had the recommended health-screening tests, and ask to see the relevant certificates.

- Check whether the litter is registered with your national Kennel Club.

- Ask whether the breeder will be willing to help you with advice after you have brought your puppy home.

- Be patient! Good breeders do not have litters constantly available for sale, and many may have a waiting list for their puppies.

- Never be tempted to buy a puppy because you feel sorry for him. Unfortunately, this just helps bad breeders stay in business, as more puppies will soon be born to replace the one just sold.

- Be very cautious of litters advertised in newspapers or on puppy sale websites on the Internet. The best sources of information on reputable breeders are the Cocker Spaniel breed clubs. The Kennel Club and the American Kennel Club also have details of breeders with litters available – but remember to do your own vetting on such breeders, as mentioned above.

Puppy
watching

Once the breeder you have chosen has a litter available, you will normally be invited to view the puppies, but note that many responsible breeders will not allow visitors to see them until they are over three or four weeks old.

This is due to the risk of infection being brought in and also because a new Cocker mum usually needs peace and quiet to concentrate on the hard work of looking after her puppies. Once the pups are old enough to receive visitors, breeders will often encourage you to visit several times until the puppies are ready to leave for their new homes at eight weeks old. This gives you plenty of time to get to know the breeder and their dogs, and to ask questions.

If you have young children, it is often better to visit the first time without the children. This makes it easier if you decide that there is something about the breeder or the litter you do not feel comfortable with. It is much harder to walk away, despite your misgivings, if your children have already seen the puppies and fallen in love with them.

When viewing a litter for the first time, there are several things you should be looking out for:

- Are the conditions where the puppies are living clean? As puppies need to toilet frequently, it is impossible to avoid a little odor sometimes, but there should be no overpowering smell and bedding should be clean and recently washed. Water bowls should be clean and contain fresh water.

- Do the puppies look healthy and happy? Healthy, well-reared pups will have sturdy, well-rounded bodies – not skinny but not too fat either – and will have clear eyes and sweet-smelling ears with no sign of discharge. Their coats will be soft and silky to the touch and there should be no sign of scurfy, itchy skin. Once at the active stage, puppies should greet visitors enthusiastically and not hide away to avoid contact, which would indicate a shy temperament.

- Is mum happy to meet visitors? The mother of a newborn litter may be suspicious of strangers, out of concern for her pups, but once the litter is less dependent and the weaning process has begun, she should be happy to meet visitors and allow them to handle her puppies.

- Is the litter housed indoors or outdoors? If puppies are reared indoors, they often receive more attention from the breeder and other family members and also get used to the sights and sounds of a normal household. This will help them adapt more quickly to family life in their new homes. However, this does not mean that kennel-reared puppies cannot adapt equally well to family life if their basic temperaments are good and as long as the breeder makes the effort to socialize and play with the pups regularly.

Prospective careers

Although many people choose a Cocker purely as a family pet, some owners are looking for a Cocker for a specific purpose, such as showing or working. In such cases, the above advice is equally applicable, but there are a few extra considerations, too.

If you want to get involved in showing or working your Cocker, you must be prepared to do some further research and make sure the breeders you contact have the type of dog you are looking for and also the necessary experience to guide you towards a puppy with the potential to succeed in your chosen activity.

If you want to show your Cocker, you will need to find a breeder that actively shows their own dogs and is successful. As mentioned earlier, there are many breeders of show-type dogs, but puppies bred by those who breed purely for the pet market will not necessarily be of the standard required for the show ring. Of course, it is never possible to guarantee that any promising puppy will grow up to be a successful show dog, but if you choose the right breeder, he or she should be able to advise which puppies show the most potential.

It takes an expert to evaluate show potential.

If you are looking to work your dog, then the same advice applies: find a breeder who works his dogs successfully and has the experience to guide you in your choice of pup. As with show dogs, there can never be a guarantee that every Working Cocker pup will make a good worker, but buying from an experienced breeder will give you a head start at least.

Making the choice

When it comes to choosing your puppy, you may find that an experienced breeder will guide you towards one whose personality will, hopefully, suit your family best. This can be very helpful, as it is often a difficult decision to pick just one from several, equally delightful, puppies.

If you are invited to make your own choice, it is tempting to pick the boldest puppy, the one that comes to you first, pushing his littermates aside. However, the boldest puppy with the pushy personality can be quite challenging if you are an inexperienced owner. In this situation, you would be better off choosing a more middle-of-the-road pup – one that is not too bold but not shy either.

A cocker-friendly home

You need to plan ahead before you collect your pup, so you have all the equipment, food and toys ready for your new arrival. You will also need to make sure your home and garden are safe and secure. These preparations apply to a new puppy but, in reality, they are the means of creating an environment that is safe and secure for your Cocker Spaniel throughout his life.

In the garden

It is important for your puppy to have access to a safe, secure space outside to make house-training easier and to give him room to play. Before you bring your pup home, check that your garden is totally secure.

Puppies can squeeze through the smallest gaps, so make sure your fencing is in good repair and is high enough for an adult Cocker (as a guide, a 5ft/1.5m fence will offer the necessary security). If you have a garden pond, either fence it off temporarily, or make sure it is covered so your puppy cannot fall in accidentally.

Cocker puppies often love to chew plants and dig holes in the garden. If you are very proud of your garden and have a number of precious shrubs or plants, it can help to protect individual plants or temporarily fence off a part of the garden just for the puppy's use.

Caution is also needed if your garden contains plants or shrubs that are poisonous when eaten by dogs. There is not the room to list all such plants here. Common examples include the laburnum tree, rhododendron, daffodil and crocus bulbs. You can find a full list on www.dogbooksonline.co.uk On a similar note, ensure all dangerous garden chemicals are kept securely locked away where your puppy cannot reach them.

In the home

As well as making sure your garden is safe, you will need to ensure that your house is as puppy-proofed as possible. This means making sure any dangling cables are safely secured and any other hazards, such as potentially poisonous houseplants or household cleaners/medicines, are well out of a puppy's reach.

If your children are in the habit of leaving their toys lying around, teach them to pick them up and store them in a toy box, particularly if they play with small plastic models, which could be easily swallowed by a puppy.

You might also want to invest in a safety gate to stop your puppy from going upstairs; young puppies should not be encouraged to run up and down stairs or steep steps, as it can be damaging for their immature growth plates. Safety gates are also useful if your house has an open-plan layout, as you can use one to block off your puppy's access to any room containing expensive carpets or furniture, at least until he is house-trained and past the chewing phase.

Finding a vet

Finding the right veterinary practice is very important for new puppy owners. Often the best way to find a good vet is to ask for recommendations from other dog-owning family members or friends/neighbors. Check what facilities are on offer, whether the staff members seem friendly and approachable and whether the opening hours are convenient for you.

You also need to find out what kind of 24-hour cover is provided for emergencies. Some practices use their own vets to provide emergency cover; others will share cover with neighboring practices. The advantage of in-house emergency cover is that you will, hopefully, see someone who already knows you and your dog if you need to call the vet out of hours.

Buying equipment

There is a vast array of different products on the market aimed at new puppy owners. Not all are essential, but here are the most important items your puppy will need:

Indoor crate

Crates are now very popular, and, when used correctly, they can help in house-training as well as providing your puppy with his own cosy 'den' in the house.

A crate needs to be somewhere a puppy feels safe and secure so you need to make it as attractive as possible, with soft bedding, some toys and perhaps a cover over the top to make it even cosier. You should also feed your pup his meals in the crate and throw treats in there from time to time.

There is a lot to do before your puppy arrives home.

Never use a crate as a means of punishment, and do not confine your puppy for lengthy periods, except when he is using it overnight.

Bed

You may decide you need a bed in addition to a crate. It is best to opt for the hard, plastic variety available in many colors and sizes. Plastic beds are easily cleaned and can be lined with a comfy, soft blanket or a piece of the popular polyester fleece bedding. They are also more durable and less likely to be chewed than fabric beds, bean-bags or the traditional wicker basket.

Bowls

Your Cocker will require one bowl for his food and one for water. There are various types of bowls available, ranging from easily-washed plastic and stainless steel to heavy pottery/stoneware bowls. Heavier bowls are best for water, as they are not easily picked up and moved around. Your puppy will only need a small food bowl to begin with, but as he gets bigger and his ears grow longer, you could invest in a spaniel bowl. Spaniel bowls are taller than average bowls and are designed with tapered sides so that the ears drop either side of the bowl, rather than dangling in the food (as is often the case with flatter bowls).

Collar/leash

Puppy collars and leashes are available in a range of colors and materials to suit all tastes. Nylon collars may be best for puppies, as these often offer more room for expansion as the puppy grows, compared to traditional leather collars. They are also washable, lightweight and are not easily chewed. Matching leashes are usually available when buying this kind of collar.

A growing puppy needs a place where he can rest undisturbed.

When buying a first leash for your puppy (whether leather or nylon), make sure it is not too long – a shorter leash is better for puppies and will give you more control when leash training.

Toys

Many owners buy a multitude of expensive toys but find their puppies prefer the homemade variety! Empty plastic bottles and cardboard boxes will often keep a puppy entertained for hours, although the owner will need to carefully supervise and remove such items once they start to disintegrate.

Puppies often like soft, furry toys too, but care must be taken to remove any easily-swallowed plastic parts first. It is best to avoid giving soft toys to your puppy if you have children with similar toys, as your pup will not be able to tell the difference between the two.

Other types of toy that your pup may enjoy include rope tug toys and nylon bones (which can help when teething), balls (but not too small to avoid the risk of your puppy accidentally swallowing one) and rubber activity toys like Kongs (which can be filled with tasty treats to keep your pup occupied for longer).

Grooming equipment

A puppy grooming kit should include a slicker brush, which is a square or rectangular brush with metal pins. It is better to buy a soft slicker to begin with, as these are kinder on a puppy's more delicate skin. You will also need two combs, one with medium-spaced teeth and one with fine teeth. A pair of straight-edged scissors (for trimming excess hair from around your puppy's feet) is also useful.

The Cocker has a soft mouth and enjoys toys he can retrieve.

Settling in

Introducing a new Cocker puppy into the family is exciting but it can also be quite daunting if you are new to puppy ownership. The information below will help you prepare for your new arrival and ensure the initial settling-in period goes as smoothly as possible.

It is better to collect your puppy from the breeder as early in the day as possible, especially if you are travelling some distance. This means your puppy will have plenty of time to adjust to his new home and get to know his new family before it is time for bed. This should make it easier for him to settle on his first night.

Meeting the family

It is a big step for any puppy to leave the security of his breeder and his existing canine family, so be prepared for it to take some time for your puppy to settle into his new home. Try not to overwhelm him with too much noise and excitement to begin with.

If you have children, they will be very excited at welcoming a new puppy and will want to pick him up and hold him. But puppies often do not enjoy being picked up, and it can also be dangerous if a child walks around while holding a puppy. Puppies squirm and wriggle and could easily fall to the ground, resulting in injury.

Encourage your children to hold the puppy when they are sitting down. Also teach them that puppies get tired very easily so they should never disturb a pup if he is sleeping.

You may have other family members and friends who are keen to come and meet your new arrival. Meeting new people is an important part in your puppy's socialization, but try to ensure he is not overwhelmed with visitors during his settling-in period, as this could be exhausting for a pup already adjusting to so many other new experiences.

Introducing house pets

If you already have an older dog, it is best to introduce your new pup on reasonably neutral territory. If the pup is too young to have been vaccinated, your garden would be the best place for introductions to take place. Ideally, put your pup in the garden and then let the resident dog out to find him, under close

supervision. Once they have been introduced, both dogs can come into the house together.

Sometimes a resident dog will accept a new puppy immediately and will be keen to play with the new arrival. Care should be taken that play sessions are not allowed to become too rough, as a bigger dog could accidentally injure a young pup during over-boisterous play.

On the other hand, a resident dog may, initially, be very suspicious of a new puppy and may take weeks to fully accept the 'incomer'. If this happens, you should be patient and ensure the older dog always has his own space where he can get some peace and quiet away from the puppy. Contact between the two should be carefully supervised during this time.

Care should also be taken when introducing a puppy to a home with other resident pets. If you have a cat or cats, they need to have an area where they can get away from the puppy if necessary. This could mean putting a stair gate across the stairs so that your cat/s can get upstairs but the pup cannot. You will also need to ensure that cat feeding bowls and litter trays are placed where your puppy cannot reach them.

Small pets, such as rabbits and guinea pigs, are best kept in secure pens or runs when you have a new puppy. Puppies can be taught not to chase small pets, but this will take time and it is best not to take any chances initially. If your small pets are used to spending short periods running around outside their pens, then they can still do this, but your pup will need to be safely contained, perhaps behind a safety gate or in a dog crate.

Do not make any changes in diet while your puppy is settling in.

Feeding

A reputable breeder will supply new owners with a detailed diet sheet, giving information on food, suggested amounts and meal timings. Most will also provide a small supply of food so that the puppy can continue to eat what he is used to during the settling-in period in a new home. This helps to avoid stomach upsets and offers the pup some continuity at a time when everything else is changing.

If you wish to change your puppy's food, it is best to wait a week at least and then gradually start mixing the new food with the old food over

a period of a few days. A sudden change of diet can result in stomach upsets.

The first night

Puppies need time to adjust to sleeping without the company of their littermates in a totally new environment. Breeders often supply an old piece of bedding and perhaps a soft toy, which smell familiar to the pup. If you place these in your pup's bed or crate, they can be very comforting and help your pup to sleep in his new home.

The old-fashioned approach to a puppy's first night – and one still popular with some owners – is to decide where the puppy will sleep, usually in a kitchen or utility room, and then put him to bed and ignore cries or howls of distress for however long it takes for the pup to fall asleep.

This approach will work eventually, but it is arguably unnecessarily harsh and could also lead to neighbor problems if you live in a modern house with thin walls. A puppy that is left to howl will also invariably make a mess overnight, as distress increases the urge to go to the toilet.

A more sympathetic approach is to decide where your puppy will sleep as before, but commit to getting up once or twice in the night so that pup can go outside to relieve himself. If you are doing this, avoid making a big fuss of your pup, as this will encourage him to be clingy and demand your company.

Calmly and quickly take your pup outside and then put him straight back to bed afterwards without fussing him or playing with him. If your puppy continues to cry, even after being outside, try not to go back down to him unless this is unavoidable. If you go to him every time he cries, he will quickly learn that this is a guaranteed way of getting your attention.

House training

This is the part that most first-time owners find daunting, but it does not need to be an ordeal if you work at it over the first few weeks, establishing a routine so your puppy understands what is required.

Young puppies have little bladder control to start off with and short attention spans. They do not always remember where they are supposed to toilet and are not capable of controlling their bladders or bowels for long periods. You need to do the thinking for your puppy, giving him every opportunity to get it right.

Getting started

The best plan is to allocate an area in your garden for toileting, and take your puppy to this spot every time you think he needs to relieve himself. This will help him to build an association so that he knows

what is expected of him, and it will also making clearing up easier.

A puppy needs to relieve himself at frequent intervals. These include:

- First thing in the morning

- Last thing at night

- After mealtimes

- Following a play session

- If the pup has been excited or stressed.

Never leave it longer than two hours between trips out to the garden; you will increase your chances of success if you take your pup outside on an hourly basis for the first few days. It can feel at this stage that you are always taking your puppy outside, but this hard work will pay off in the long run, providing you are consistent.

Here are a few key things to remember:

- Do not expect your puppy to train himself by leaving the door open or just letting him outside while you stay inside. You must go outside with your puppy (whatever the weather) and wait with him until he does the necessary.

- Use a key phrase every time you want your puppy to go to the toilet. This phrase, such as "Hurry up" or "Be quick", will eventually become associated in your pup's mind with toileting outside and you will be able to use it to command your puppy to 'go' wherever you are – at home or on a walk.

- Praise your puppy quietly for toileting in the right place. It is important to reward good behavior, so use your voice to praise or offer a small treat, but do not go overboard or your pup will get over excited.

When accidents happen

Never punish your puppy if you discover an accident in the home. It is in order to calmly but firmly say "No, outside" if you catch your pup doing a puddle inside. But it is pointless and cruel to punish a puppy for something that he did even minutes ago, as he will have no idea why you are cross.

Clean up any accidents calmly and without fuss. Remember to use either biological washing detergent or specialist urine cleaner rather than normal household disinfectants, as these may contain ammonia, which can attract puppies back to the same spot.

Choosing
a diet

A healthy Cocker needs a balanced diet that contains the right amount of proteins, fats, carbohydrates, fiber, vitamins and minerals. However, there is no single diet available that is guaranteed to suit every Cocker for the whole of his life.

Just like humans, dogs are all individuals and what suits one dog may not suit another. A dog's dietary needs may change according to his age and his lifestyle – for example, a growing, active puppy needs a very different diet to an elderly, less active dog. The important thing is to find the right diet that suits your Cocker at each relevant stage of his life.

Commercial dog diets

Complete dry foods have become very popular for reasons of cost and convenience. Owners like the

fact they can just pour the appropriate amount of kibble in their dog's bowl with minimum fuss and effort. Many Cockers enjoy complete dry dog foods and thrive on this type of diet. However, it has to be said that not all dry dog foods are equal. There can be a considerable difference in the quality of ingredients of a cheaper brand compared to a more expensive, premium brand.

As with most things, you get what you pay for. A good-quality complete food may appear more expensive initially, but you will usually have to feed less than you would a cheaper brand because the food has better, more easily digestible ingredients.

Check the ingredients listed on the bag and look for a food with a high content of real meat, with a named protein source (chicken, lamb, fish etc) as the first ingredient, and as few additives as possible. These are signs of a good-quality food that uses the best ingredients to keep your Cocker healthy and happy.

Some owners prefer to feed a 'wet' food, supplied in sealed pouches or cans, as these are often more palatable to dogs, particularly if you have a fussy eater. However, it again pays to check the ingredients list, as some cans or pouches contain artificial colors and additives and have a high sugar content.

Natural diets

At one time, the traditional way of feeding a dog was to mix raw or cooked meat with a biscuit meal or perhaps with rice. Vegetable scraps from the family table would often also be added. Many dogs lived long, happy lives on this kind of diet and there is no reason why owners today cannot continue to feed a home-prepared diet along these lines.

There is certainly an argument that the use of freshly prepared, more natural ingredients is better for the health of dogs, just as it is for humans. However, care must be taken to ensure a home-prepared diet offers the right balance of vitamins and minerals.

The BARF (bones and raw food, or biologically appropriate raw food) diet goes further than the home-prepared traditional diet and involves feeding purely raw food and bones, replicating the diet of a wild dog as far as possible.

If this is something that interests you, then do your research first so you have a good basic grounding on what you will need to raise your Cocker on this diet.

Feeding regime

How often you feed your Cocker will depend on his age. Puppies leaving for their new homes at eight weeks old will usually be on four meals a day. At this age, their stomachs are small and so they need small meals spaced out over the day. Generally, it is best to leave around four hours between meals to give time for each meal to be digested.

As puppies grow, their stomachs can take bigger meals and it becomes possible to reduce the frequency of meal times. From four months old, most puppies will be on three meals a day and this then goes down to two meals at six months old and onwards.

Traditionally, many dogs were only fed once a day when they reached adulthood, from 12 months onwards, but owners often find that their adult Cockers are happier continuing on a regime of two meals a day, usually fed morning and late afternoon or evening.

It is better to provide set meal times for your dog, as free feeding, where a bowl of food is left down all day long and is continually topped up, can encourage over-eating and make it very difficult to monitor how much a dog is actually eating, particularly in a home with more than one dog. Fixed meal times also make it easier to predict when your dog needs to go outside to toilet; bowel movements often follow a meal, especially in young puppies.

How much to feed?

How much to feed your Cocker will depend on various factors, such as his age, whether he is neutered, and how active he is. Growing puppies need relatively more food than they will as adults to ensure optimum development. Neutered Cockers can be prone to weight gain so may need less food than before and, perhaps, a change in diet to one of the specially formulated low-calorie dog foods. The same applies to older Cockers, who become less active as they age and so need less food; they also need a lower level of protein than is found in foods aimed at young dogs.

Most Cockers thrive on a regime of two meals a day.

On the other hand, very active dogs, such as working dogs or those that take part in activities such as agility, may need an increase in the amount fed and perhaps a diet with higher levels of fat and protein to maintain their energy levels and optimum weight.

If you are feeding a commercial dog food, the manufacturer will supply information on suggested feeding amounts per age of puppy/dog, but this should be treated as a rough guide only.   You also need to take into account any treats you give during training sessions, as these need to be included in your Cocker's daily allowance, particularly if he is prone to weight gain.

Assessing your Cocker's weight

If your Cocker is carrying the right amount of weight – not too fat and not too thin – you should be able to feel your dog's ribs but not see them, and he should have a noticeable waist with his body narrowing slightly after the ribs.

If you cannot easily feel the ribs, then it may be time to reduce the amount fed; if the ribs are too prominent and your dog feels overly bony along the spine, you may need to increase his food.

Bones and chews

There is a huge variety of commercially prepared bones and chews on the market, ranging from beef hide chews to hard, plastic bones. If you are buying rawhide chews for your Cocker, it is best to go for the larger, pressed type, as these will not be so easily swallowed and destroyed.

Raw marrow bones are also enjoyed by many dogs but are perhaps best not given to young puppies, as they can be too rich for their stomachs. Never feed cooked bones to your dog, as cooking makes bones brittle and prone to splintering, which can be very dangerous.

Keep a close check on your Cocker to ensure he does not gain excess weight.

Caring for your Cocker

The Cocker is a long-haired breed and so needs regular grooming to keep the coat knot-free and in good condition. Show-type Cockers have thicker, longer coats than working type dogs, but all Cockers will need to learn to accept being groomed on a regular basis.

Puppy grooming

Start your grooming routine as soon as your puppy comes home so that he gets used to the idea long before his coat is thick enough to require extensive grooming.

Always groom your Cocker on a raised surface or table otherwise you may find that you have to chase him around the floor on your hands and knees, which is not conducive to a successful grooming session! Make sure the surface of your table is non-slip by

placing either a rubber mat or small piece of carpet on the top. This is not necessary if you invest in a purpose-made grooming table.

Spend a few minutes every day gently brushing your puppy all over with a slicker brush. Reward your puppy for standing still, even if it is just for a few seconds at first. Eventually, he will stand for longer periods, but it will take patience and lots of practice before this is achieved, so you will need to persevere.

Teach your puppy to lie on his back while you brush under his elbows and in the groin area, where knots often appear as the coat grows. Comb through his ears and also check his nails to see if they need clipping. You can use ordinary 'human' nail clippers for puppy nails, but you will need to invest in dog nail clippers for adult nails.

As your puppy grows, his coat will usually grow thicker and longer, particularly if he comes from show lines. This means he will need a more thorough grooming session – perhaps 10 to 15 minutes a day. You should comb through the ear and body feathering, using your medium-toothed comb, to ensure there are no knots left anywhere. You can also use your slicker brush to remove any loose hair from the topcoat or to brush out small tangles from the feathering.

Puppy feet can become quite hairy, so you should use your small scissors to trim excess hair from under and around the foot. You could also check inside the ears and use your scissors to snip away excess hair.

Eventually, many show-type Cocker puppies will reach a stage where more extensive trimming is needed over and above regular daily grooming. When this time comes, usually at five to six months of age onwards, you will need to decide which type of trim is most suitable for you and your Cocker.

If you teach your Cocker to roll over, it will make grooming easier.

Show trim

Show Cockers are trimmed using the traditional method of hand stripping, where excess dead hair is plucked out, using finger and thumb, or stripped out with a small, fine-toothed comb, often known as a spaniel comb.

This is a long process, requiring a considerable degree of skill, but it produces a lovely, natural finish, which lasts longer than other methods. Patience is needed, as coats can only be stripped out when the hair is ready to come out naturally, which can be as late as nine months or even older in some dogs.

Clippers and other tools with blades should never be used on show Cockers, as they cut the coat and result in an unnatural finish. Feathering under the body and on the legs and ears is left long but will be shaped and thinned out where necessary with thinning scissors. Straight-edged scissors are used to keep the feet tidy.

If you want to show your Cocker or you would like your pet Cocker to be trimmed in the traditional way, you may need to learn how to hand strip your dog yourself, as very few professional groomers are

Below: It takes a lot of hard work to keep a Cocker in show trim.

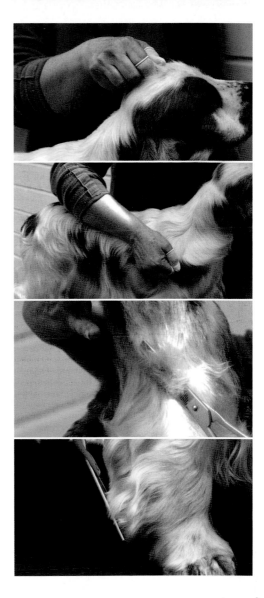

Hand-stripping, using finger and thumb, is needed to remove the dead hair.

You need to work down the length of the body.

Trimming with thinning scissors helps the coat to lie flat.

Straight scissors are used to tidy up the feathering.

able to provide this service due to the time it takes. However, some Cocker breeders and exhibitors do provide a hand stripping service or are willing to offer tuition to a keen newcomer. Failing that, there are grooming videos and booklets available, which offer advice and demonstrate the necessary techniques.

Pet trim

A sympathetic pet trim for both Cocker types involves removing excess body hair with either a combination of thinning scissors and stripping tools, or with electric clippers. Clippers do a quick, efficient job, but the effect is less natural than the scissors/stripping tool approach. Feathering is thinned out and trimmed much shorter than for a show dog.

If you opt for a pet trim for your Cocker, you can buy the necessary tools and learn to do this yourself, which saves money in the long run, or you can pay for a professional groomer's services. You will need to visit a professional groomer every eight to 12 weeks and, as with other canine services, it pays to do your homework and find one by personal recommendation if possible.

Electric clippers are used for a pet trim.

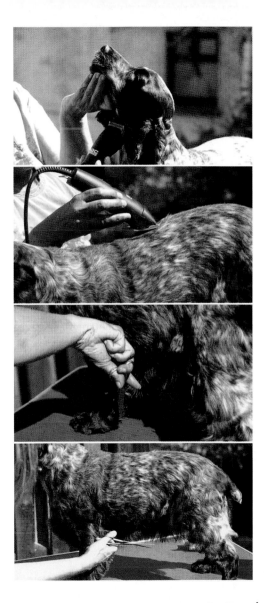

Again, you need to work down the length of the body.

Feathering needs to be trimmed.

The longer hair on the underside will also need to be tidied.

Bathing

There is no hard-and-fast rule about how often you should bath your Cocker. As a general guide, bath your dog when you feel he needs it, particularly if he is very muddy or has rolled in something particularly unpleasant, as Cockers often do. Do not be afraid to bath your puppy. Getting a young puppy used to the sensation of being bathed and the noise of the hairdryer means these experiences will hold no fear for him as he grows up.

Regular checks

During your regular daily grooming sessions, you should practise opening and examining your puppy's mouth, inspecting his ears, and touching his feet and nails, including any dew claws situated inside the leg above the foot.

This will be very useful in the future, as your Cocker will be used to being handled and will accept veterinary examinations when necessary without any fuss. It also means you will be immediately alerted to any problems that might need attention – for example, discharge from the ear, indicating an ear infection.

Grooming and checking the ear feathering regularly will also help you to spot any grass seeds picked up in your dog's feathering in the summer months.

Accustom your Cocker to teeth cleaning from an early age.

Wipe the debris from the eyes.

Ear cleaning is very important for Cockers.

Nails need trimming on a routine basis.

These seeds can cause intense pain and irritation if they find their way into the ear canal.

Neutering and the Cocker coat

Neutering results in hormonal changes that can affect the coats of many Cockers, including working-strain dogs. These changes can take months to be noticeable, but owners will often find that coats become thicker and coarser, and, eventually, hand stripping ceases to be an option, as the coat no longer comes out naturally. When this happens, the usual solution is to use electric clippers to keep the coat neat and tidy.

Exercise

The amount of exercise your Cocker will need depends largely on how old he is and also whether he is a show-type or a working-type dog.

Young puppies should not be over-exercised, as this can put too much strain on immature joints and growth plates, resulting in arthritis in later life and possibly contributing to the development of hip dysplasia in genetically susceptible dogs.

For puppies, a good general guide is to allow five minutes of formal exercise per month of age until fully grown. For a four-month-old puppy, this would mean that walks should last for about 20 minutes.

Two short walks a day combined with play sessions in the garden are normally more than sufficient for a puppy of this age. As your pup gets older, you can gradually increase the length of his walks, still following the five-minute rule until he is fully grown at around 10 months of age.

Adult Cockers can usually take as much exercise as their owner is willing to provide, although, of course, there should be a gradual build-up to any really long-distance hikes. Many show-type Cockers will happily accept two moderate walks a day (30-40 minutes each approximately) with perhaps longer walks at weekends and during the holidays. These walks should include some opportunity for off-lead exercise, as there is nothing a Cocker likes more than to use his nose to investigate all the interesting scents in fields and parks.

Working Cockers may need considerably more daily exercise; if this is not provided, they can become bored and frustrated. Although this is something of a generalization, as all Cockers are individuals, it needs to be considered if you have a dog from working lines.

Fun and games

Exercise does not just mean walking your Cocker on the lead or letting him run about in a field. You can also play interactive games with your dog, which will exercise his body and provide mental stimulation too. Mental stimulation is very important for a busy, intelligent breed like a Cocker and will help relieve boredom and make for a calm, relaxed dog.

As a gundog breed, many Cockers naturally like to pick up items and bring them to you. You can harness this instinct by throwing balls or Frisbees and teaching your dog to retrieve them. You can also play hide and seek in the garden or in the house on a wet day. Hide dog treats or scatter a portion of your dog's daily food (if feeding a kibble) around the garden; your Cocker will happily entertain himself, rooting out the hidden treasure!

The older Cocker

Cockers can remain healthy and active well into their senior years although some adjustments to diet may be necessary as time goes on.

A light or senior food may be more suitable for an older Cocker if he is not as active as he was once was and particularly if he is neutered, when weight gain may be an issue. Supplements such as fish oil can also be useful for the older Cocker that is becoming a little arthritic in his movement.

The older Cocker will also usually appreciate a waterproof coat on wet walks and a soft, supportive bed in a draft-free area of the house.

It is a good idea to regularly check your dog's skin and coat as he ages, as older Cockers can be prone to lumps and bumps on their bodies. These are usually non-malignant fatty lumps (lipomas) and can often be safely left alone. However, all lumps should be checked out by a vet as a precaution.

Older Cockers should continue to be exercised for as long as they enjoy it, although they may be happier with shorter walks than before. A very elderly Cocker may no longer want to go out for formal walks but will be content with a regular potter around the garden.

Facing page: Be aware of the changing needs of your Cocker as he grows older.

Older dogs also need to keep their brains active, so it is important to continue to play games and offer toys as before. There are even specially designed toys for senior dogs, generally made of softer material for dogs not able to chew as hard as in their youth.

Letting go

Inevitably there will come a time when you realize that your Cocker is no longer enjoying life as he once did, either because of serious illness or simply due to the frailty of old age. Knowing when is the right time to let go of a beloved pet is one of the most difficult decisions any owner will ever have to make.

Some owners find the decision so hard that they leave it too long, and, as a result, their dog suffers unnecessarily, although this is not the owner's intention. Remember that your Cocker has given you years of companionship and unconditional affection, and, in return, he deserves to be given a dignified, peaceful ending – no matter how difficult this might be for you.

The signs that the time has come to make that decision are when the bad days far outweigh the good, when you can see your Cocker has little interest in life any more, or when he is in pain more often than he is not. You may find he no longer wants his food and prefers to stay in his bed all day, reluctant to move. Even a very ill Cocker will still try to wag his tail and lift his head to greet his family, but when this is an obvious effort, listen to what he is telling you and have the strength to make that final telephone call to your vet.

The vet may come to your home so that your dog's last moments are as peaceful and stress-free as possible, which is particularly important if you have a Cocker who is anxious about visiting the surgery.

Saying goodbye to your Cocker will be very upsetting for all members of the family, but, in time, you will have the comfort of knowing you did the kindest thing possible and will be able to look back on all those happy times you spent together.

|Social skills

Your Cocker Spaniel puppy has a lot to learn as he grows up, and it is your job to train him to be a well-behaved canine citizen who will cope calmly in all situations.

Socialization is the process of getting your puppy used to all the different sights, sounds and experiences he is likely to come across when living in our busy, modern world. The aim is to be able to take your Cocker anywhere and in any situation and for him to remain relaxed and confident at all times.

The period between three and 12 weeks is a critical time in a puppy's social development. A puppy that is kept isolated during this time may become timid and never develop the confident, happy personality expected of a family pet. Good breeders will start off the socialization process by regularly handling the pups and making sure they encounter a variety of different household noises before they leave for their new homes. However, it will be the new owner's job to continue this process.

Inside and outside the home

As part of your program to introduce your pup to a wide range of different people, you should encourage visitors to your home, including children of different ages, which is especially important if you do not have children yourself.

Introductions should be kept as relaxed as possible, so do not allow your visitors to speak or pet your puppy until he is reacting calmly and always carefully supervise encounters with children. Young children can unintentionally hurt a puppy with rough handling.

You will also need to take your pup outside the home and into neighboring streets so that he can get used to the noise of traffic. Start with a fairly quiet street and then gradually introduce busier roads as your pup becomes more confident.

Other dogs

Socialization with other dogs is essential so that your puppy grows up with good doggy manners, and is able to read other dogs' body language and communicate with them without fear or aggression.

Puppies can also learn a lot from sensible, older dogs that will teach the importance of good manners, tolerating a certain amount of rough play from youngsters but also making it clear when pups go too far. If you do not own an older dog yourself, perhaps you have friends or neighbors who have good-natured older dogs and would be happy for your puppy to be introduced to them under careful supervision.

Well-socialized dogs are calm and confident in all situations.

Ongoing socialization

Although the critical period for socialization is three to 12 weeks, socialization is not something that is over and done with once a puppy reaches a certain age. It is an ongoing process that needs to be continued and reinforced until the puppy reaches adulthood; it should then be 'topped up' throughout your Cocker's life.

Training guidelines

Training your puppy is an essential part of your responsibilities as his owner. A well-trained Cocker is a pleasure to own; he fits happily into family life and understands what is expected of him at home and when out in public.

In contrast, an untrained dog is often stressed and confused, having no understanding of how to behave. He can also be a danger to himself and to others since he is not under the control of his owner.

Training is also about teamwork and developing a deeper bond with your dog. It will help you to develop a close relationship with your Cocker, resulting in a well-mannered dog whose attention is focussed on you – most of the time!

When you are training, try to stick to the following guidelines to give you, and your Cocker, the best chance of success:

- Find a reward your Cocker really wants. This could be a toy or food, depending on the individual.

- If you are using food, you can vary the reward so you have high value treats (cheese or sausage) for teaching new exercises and recalls away from home, and low value treats (dry kibble) for routine training.

- If you are using a toy as a reward, make sure you only bring it out for training sessions so it has added value.

- Work on your tone of voice. This will be far more meaningful to your Cocker than the words you are saying. Use a bright, happy, upbeat tone when you are training, and a deep, firm voice when you catch him red handed – raiding the bin, for example. Go over the top when you praise your Cocker so that he understands how pleased you are with him.

- Train in short sessions. This applies particularly to puppies, which have a very short attention span, but adults will also switch off if sessions are too long.

Find a reward your Cocker wants to work for.

- Never train if you are preoccupied or if you are in a bad mood. Your Cocker will pick up on your negative vibes, and the session is doomed to disaster.

- Teach one lesson at a time and only proceed to the next lesson when the first has been mastered.

- Praise success lavishly and ignore failure. You do not have to tell your dog off if he gets it wrong. Simply ignore what he has done, and use a bright, positive tone of voice and tell him to "Try again".

- If your Cocker is struggling with an exercise, break it down into stages so you can reward him at every step, and he has a clearer understanding of what is required.

- Make sure training sessions always end on a positive note – even if this means abandoning an exercise for the time being and finishing with something you know your Cocker can do.

- Above all, make sure your training sessions are fun, with lots of play and plenty of opportunities to reward you dog, so that you both enjoy spending time together.

|First lessons

A Cocker puppy will soak up new experiences like a sponge, so training should start from the time your pup arrives in his new home. It is so much easier to teach good habits rather than trying to correct your puppy when he has established an undesirable pattern of behavior.

Wearing a collar

It is a legal requirement for a dog to wear a collar with an identity tag when out in public, so it makes sense to get your puppy used to wearing a collar before he is officially allowed outside the home, after his vaccinations.

This is usually quite easy if you start with a lightweight puppy collar and leave it on for short periods initially, and then gradually build up the time the collar is left on. Your puppy may scratch at his neck at first, but this will soon pass once he is used to the sensation of the collar around his neck.

If you are using a crate to train your puppy, you should remove his collar before shutting him inside as, sadly, there have been incidents when collars have become tangled in the wire mesh of a crate with tragic consequences.

Leash training

Make an early start on leash training so your puppy is ready to be taken out when he has completed his vaccinations.

Start by attaching a lightweight leash to his collar and let him wander around for short period with it trailing behind him. Then progress to holding the end of the lead and trying short practice walks in the garden. If your puppy is reluctant to move forwards, it can help to hold a treat out in your other hand to encourage him.

Once your puppy is comfortable wearing a leash, you can start teaching him to walk on a loose leash at your side. This is important because pulling on the leash can be a common problem for Cocker owners and the earlier you teach him not to pull, the better. Cockers have a tendency to pull because their natural exuberance means they are usually very eager to get to where they are going. They quickly realize that pulling works because their owners continue to walk on behind them, i.e. pulling is rewarded by the walk continuing.

The most effective way of training your Cocker not to pull is never to reward this behavior, meaning that you must stop moving every time he starts to pull. When you stop, your dog will usually turn round to see why he cannot move forward anymore, making the lead slacken. At this moment, you should immediately praise him and then continue walking for as long as the lead remains loose.

The process must then be repeated each and every time your dog starts to pull. This stop-start method is generally very effective but it does take considerable patience and persistence, as it can be some time before your Cocker finally gets the message that pulling gets him nowhere.

Training must suit the individual, so only progress when your Cocker is ready.

Come when called

The recall is a command every Cocker puppy needs to learn since this is a breed that can have a strong hunting instinct. This means a Cocker can sometimes be more interested in following his nose than listening to his owner.

Young puppies generally feel dependent on their owners and reluctant to wander too far from them, so it is the ideal time to start teaching the Come exercise. It becomes much more difficult when a Cocker reaches adolescence and becomes more independent and inclined to be selectively deaf to the owner's calls.

The Come exercise needs to be associated with positive experiences to make your puppy want to return to you from whatever he is doing. You can start teaching your puppy to "Come" in the garden, using tasty treats, or a favorite toy if he is not food-motivated, to reward him for responding. You can then progress to practising in other areas with more distractions.

When you are confident that your puppy understands what you want and is coming back every time you ask, you can progress.

While you are teaching your puppy to come, it can be useful to use a long training line attached to a harness, especially if you do not have access to enclosed exercise areas. This will enable your puppy to have some freedom to explore, but he will still be under your control while he is being trained.

Always use a happy but confident tone of voice and positive body language when calling your pup. For example, bending down and holding your arms out is more inviting to a dog than standing and frowning, with your arms crossed.

Make yourself exciting so that your Cocker finds you irresistible. Jump up and down, run for a few paces – it doesn't matter what you do as long as your Cocker can't wait to come back to you!

Never scold your puppy for returning to you, even if he has taken his time to respond. Shouting at a Cocker for coming back to you too slowly will guarantee that he will not bother coming at all the next time you call.

Stationary exercises

These are easy exercises to teach, so you and your Cocker will be able to enjoy a sense of achievement – without too much effort!

Sit

- You can start training this exercise with a treat, and once your puppy understands what is required you can practice at mealtimes, asking him to "Sit" before you put down his food bowl.

- Start by standing in front of your pup, holding a tasty treat. Then move the treat above your puppy's head and keep moving it slowly backwards.

- You should find that as your puppy tries to follow the treat with his eyes, his bottom will naturally hit the floor and he will sit, even if only for a second.

- When he does this, immediately reward him and give him the treat.

- Repeat this regularly, and when your puppy understands what is expected, you can introduce the verbal cue, "Sit."

- Eventually the treats can become less frequent, but you should continue to give verbal praise for a good response.

- Remember to practise in as many different places as possible so that your puppy learns to respond wherever he is.

Down

- This is an important lesson, and can be a lifesaver if an emergency arises and you need to bring your Cocker to an instant halt.

- You can start with your dog in a Sit or a Stand for this exercise. Stand or kneel in front of him and show him you have a treat in your hand.

- Hold the treat just in front of his nose and slowly lower it towards the ground, between his front legs. As he follows the treat he will go down on his front legs and, in a few moments, his hindquarters will follow.

- Close your hand over the treat so your Cocker doesn't cheat and get the treat before he is in the correct position. As soon as he is in the Down, give him the treat and lots of praise.

- Keep practising, and when your Cocker understands what you want, introduce the verbal cue "Down".

With practice, your Cocker will go into the "Down" without needing to be lured into position.

Control exercises

The Cocker Spaniel is a livewire and likes nothing better than to be on the move, investigating every sight, sound and smell. However, it is important to introduce some measure of control so he learns to inhibit his natural exuberance when required.

Stay

Once your puppy has mastered the Sit command, you can start to teach him the Stay, meaning he must stay where he is until you say he can move.

Start by telling your puppy to "Sit" and slowly move one step back from him. Return to him straight away, give him a treat and praise him softly. Do not overdo the praise, as you want your pup to remain calm. Repeat this process, but wait a second or two before returning, then progress to moving two steps

away. At this stage, you can introduce the verbal command "Stay", gradually increasing the time you wait before returning to your pup and the number of steps you move away from him. This will take time, so try not to rush things or become frustrated if your puppy cannot seem to stay still for more than a second or two at first.

If your puppy breaks the stay before you come back with the treat, then just go back to the beginning and start again, always aiming to end your training session on a good note. You should start to see steady improvement if you practise this exercise little and often.

Wait

The Wait command is different to the Stay, as the aim is to make him pause briefly before you give another command, e.g. waiting at the side of the road before crossing over or waiting while you open the front door.

You will find your Cocker will pick this command up very quickly if you practise your Wait command in a calm, assertive voice at times when he is anticipating something enjoyable, such as a meal or going out for a walk. When you are getting his food bowl ready, give the Sit command and do not put the bowl down until he has waited for a couple of seconds. You can

then say, "Okay" – your cue to tell your dog that he can now eat his food. When your puppy understands what is required, introduce the verbal cue "Wait".

Teaching "no" and "leave"

"No" is often used by owners to interrupt an unwanted behavior, such as when your Cocker is chewing something potentially dangerous, but the tone of your voice is more important than the word chosen.

Instead of "No", many owners find that saying something like "Ah ah" in a sharp voice is more effective at getting a dog's attention and stopping him in his tracks. Once you have done this, it is not enough to simply interrupt the behavior, otherwise he could go straight back to doing it. You need to direct him towards a more positive activity – for example, offering one of his own safe toys to chew or asking him to do a simple exercise such as Sit or a Down, so you can reward his 'good' behavior.

Teaching your puppy to "Leave" items on command is very important, especially as some Cockers have a tendency to be possessive over things they pick up. If your Cocker picks up an item you do not want him to have, it can be tempting to simply grab him and forcibly try to remove the item from his mouth. Unfortunately, this often has the effect of making a dog defend his 'treasure', making him even more possessive the next time he finds something he wants to keep to himself.

The best way to teach your puppy to leave items on command is to either play a game of swap, where you offer a favorite toy in exchange for the forbidden item, or to use high-value treats – an extra-tasty titbit – so that your Cocker learns that something very enjoyable comes his way if he leaves his 'treasure'.

Rather than confronting your Cocker, offer him another toy as a swap.

The ideal owner

You want to do the very best you can for your Cocker Spaniel, and give him a rewarding and fulfilling life. But in order to do this, you need to make sure you fully understand his needs.

The ideal owner knows that the Cocker is not just a pretty face; he is a busy, active dog needing plenty of exercise, human companionship and interesting activities to keep his brain occupied.

He is intelligent and eager to learn, but he can sometimes be stubborn and quick to take advantage of an over-indulgent owner who treats him like a baby. A Cocker needs boundaries for acceptable behavior, and it is your duty to provide them.

The ideal owner provides patient, consistent training from the start, with the aim of building a partnership based on mutual trust and respect. The effort involved will be amply rewarded when you own a happy, confident Cocker that fits well into family life and is a joy to own.

Opportunities for Cockers

The Cocker is a very versatile breed and there are many activities that owners can enjoy with their dogs, whether at a basic fun level or at a more serious competitive level. Here are some of the most popular activities for Cockers.

Working

As the Cocker was developed as a working gundog breed, it can be enormously satisfying to train your dog to fulfil his original function in the field, and your Cocker will enjoy it, too. If you want to train your dog to work, you will need to join a gundog club or obtain the services of a one-to-one gundog trainer.

While show-type Cockers can enjoy gundog training and become competent working dogs, only working Cockers will have the drive and stamina needed to reach the standard required for high level field trial competitions. So if your ambitions lie in this direction,

you will need a Cocker bred from successful working lines rather than a show-type dog.

Good Citizen Scheme

The Good Citizen Scheme is run by the national Kennel Clubs in both the USA and the UK, and is designed to promote responsible ownership and to teach basic obedience and good manners so your dog is a model citizen in the community.

In the US there is one test; in the UK there are four award levels – Puppy Foundation, Bronze, Silver and Gold.

The scheme also provides a solid foundation for owners interested in moving on to competitive obedience, or to field trial training if you have a working Cocker.

The show ring

If you intend to show your puppy, you will need to attend ringcraft classes so you train your dog to perform in the ring and you can also learn about show ring etiquette

Bear in mind that working Cockers cannot be exhibited at formal dog shows, but you can attend Companion shows and other fun events. Championship shows are the most prestigious and this is where show-bred Cocker spaniels compete to become Show Champions.

Showing is great fun, but at the top level it is highly competitive, so you will need to learn the art of winning – and losing – gracefully.

Agility

This is a fun sport where dogs complete an obstacle course against the clock. Both strains of Cocker enjoy agility, although owners need to be fit, as this is a very fast-moving activity. At competition level, speed is important, and, in recent years, Working Cockers have become very popular agility dogs – they are usually faster than their show cousins.

The Cocker is a willing pupil and will enjoy the challenge of advanced training.

If you are interested in agility with your Cocker, you will need to find an agility club where you and your dog will be taught the skills needed, but you will not be able to start training until your Cocker is 12 months old, as dogs need to be fully grown. Some owners are happy just to take part in weekly agility training sessions, but if want to take it to a competitive level and enter agility shows, your Cocker needs to be 18 months old and he also has to be formally measured to determine the size category he will compete in – Cockers are either Small or Medium.

Competitive obedience

This is a sport where you are assessed as a dog and handler, completing a series of exercises including heelwork, recalls, retrieves, stays, sendaways and scent discrimination.

The Cocker is quick to learn and likes to please, so he more than capable of learning and performing the exercises. These are relatively simple to begin with, involving heelwork, a recall and stays in the lowest class, and, as your progress through, more exercises are added, and the aids you are allowed to give are reduced.

To achieve top honors in this discipline requires intensive training as precision and accuracy are of paramount importance.

Health care

We are fortunate that the Cocker Spaniel is a healthy dog, with no exaggerations, and with good routine care, a well-balanced diet, and sufficient exercise, most dogs will experience few health problems.

However, it is your responsibility to put a program of preventative health care in place – and this should start from the moment your puppy, or older dog, arrives in his new home.

Vaccinations

Dogs are subject to a number of contagious diseases. In the old days, these were killers, and resulted in heartbreak for many owners. Vaccinations have now been developed, and the occurrence of the major infectious diseases is now very rare. However, this will only remain the case if all pet owners follow a strict policy of vaccinating their dogs.

Dogs are subject to a number of contagious diseases. In the old days, these were killers, and resulted in heartbreak for many owners. Vaccinations have now been developed, and the occurrence of the major infectious diseases is now very rare. However, this will only remain the case if all pet owners follow a strict policy of vaccinating their dogs.

There are vaccinations available for the following diseases:

Adenovirus: This affects the liver; affected dogs have a classic 'blue eye'.

Distemper: A viral disease which causes chest and gastro-intestinal damage. The brain may also be affected, leading to fits and paralysis.

Parvovirus: Causes severe gastro enteritis, and most commonly affects puppies.

Leptospirosis: This bacterial disease is carried by rats and affects many mammals, including humans. It causes liver and kidney damage.

Rabies: A virus that affects the nervous system and is invariably fatal. The first signs are abnormal behavior when the infected dog may bite another animal or a person. Paralysis and death follow. Vaccination is compulsory in most countries. In the UK, dogs travelling overseas must be vaccinated.

Kennel Cough: There are several strains of Kennel Cough, but they all result in a harsh, dry, cough. This disease is rarely fatal; in fact most dogs make a good recovery within a matter of weeks and show few signs of ill health while they are affected. However, kennel cough is highly infectious among dogs that live together so, for this reason, most boarding kennels will insist that your dog is protected by the vaccine, which is given as nose drops.

Lyme Disease: This is a bacterial disease transmitted by ticks (see page 171). The first signs are limping, but the heart, kidneys and nervous system can also be affected. The ticks that transmit the disease occur in specific regions, such as the north-east states of the USA, some of the southern states, California and the upper Mississippi region. Lyme disease is till rare in the UK so vaccinations are not routinely offered.

Vaccination program

In the UK, vaccinations are routinely given for distemper, adenovirus, leptospirosis and parvo virus. In the USA, the American Animal Hospital Association advises vaccination for core diseases, which they list as: distemper, adenovirus, parvovirus and rabies. The requirement for vaccinating for non-core diseases – leptospirosis, lyme disease and kennel cough – should be assessed depending on a dog's individual risk and his likely exposure to the disease.

Facing page: Puppies must be protected from the major contagious diseases.

In most cases, a puppy will start his vaccinations at around eight weeks of age, with the second part given in a fortnight's time. However, this does vary depending on the individual policy of veterinary practices, and the incidence of disease in your area.

You should also talk to your vet about whether to give annual booster vaccinations. This depends on an individual dog's levels of immunity, and how long a particular vaccine remains effective.

Parasites

No matter how well you look after your Cocker Spaniel, you will have to accept that parasites – internal and external – are ever present, and you need to take preventative action.

Internal parasites: As the name suggests, these parasites live inside your dog. Most will find a home in the digestive tract, but there is also a parasite that lives in the heart. If infestation is unchecked, a dog's health will be severely jeopardized, but routine preventative treatment is simple and effective.

External parasites: These parasites live on your dog's body – in his skin and fur, and sometimes in his ears.

Roundworm

This is found in the small intestine, and signs of infestation will be a poor coat, a pot belly, diarrhoea and lethargy. Pregnant mothers should be treated, but it is almost inevitable that parasites will be passed on to the puppies. For this reason, a breeder will start a worming program, which you will need to continue. Ask your vet for advice on treatment, which will need to continue throughout your dog's life.

Tapeworm

Infection occurs when fleas and lice are ingested; the adult worm takes up residence in the small intestine, releasing mobile segments (which contain eggs) which can be seen in a dog's feces as small rice-like grains. The only other obvious sign of infestation is irritation of the anus. Again, routine preventative treatment is required throughout your Cocker's life.

Heartworm

This parasite is transmitted by mosquitoes, and so will only occur where these insects thrive. A warm environment is needed for the parasite to develop, so it is more likely to be present in areas with a warm, humid climate. However, it is found in all parts of the USA, although its prevalence does vary. At present, heartworm is rarely seen in the UK.

Heartworms live in the right side of the heart and larvae can grow up to 14in (35cm) in length. A dog with heartworm is at severe risk from heart failure, so preventative treatment, as advised by your vet, is essential. Dogs living in the USA should also have regular blood tests to check for the presence of infection.

Lungworm

Lungworm, or *Angiostrongylus vasorum*, is a parasite that lives in the heart and major blood vessels supplying the lungs. It can cause many problems, such as breathing difficulties, excessive bleeding, sickness and diarrhoea, seizures, and can even be fatal. The parasite is carried by slugs and snails and their trails, and the dog becomes infected when ingesting these, often accidentally when rummaging through undergrowth. Lungworm is not common, but it is on the increase and a responsible owner should be aware of it. Fortunately, it is easily preventable and even affected dogs usually make a full recovery if treated early enough. Your vet will be able to advise you on the risks in your area and what form of treatment may be required.

Fleas

Fleas stay on the dog only long enough to have a blood meal and to breed, but their presence will result in itching and scratching. If your dog has an allergy to fleas – which is usually a reaction to the flea's saliva – he will scratch himself until he is raw.

Spot-on treatment, administered regularly, is easy to use and highly effective. You can also treat your dog with a spray or with insecticidal shampoo. Bear in mind that the whole environment and all other pets living in your home will also need to be treated.

How to detect fleas

You may suspect your dog has fleas, but how can you be sure? There are two methods to try.

Run a fine comb through your dog's coat, and see if you can detect the presence of fleas on the skin, or clinging to the comb. Alternatively, sit your dog on some white paper and rub his back. This will dislodge feces from the fleas, which will be visible as small brown specks. To double check, shake the specks on to some damp cotton wool (cotton). Flea feces consists of the dried blood taken from the host, so if the specks turn a lighter shade of red, you know your dog has fleas.

Ticks

These are blood-sucking parasites which are most frequently found in rural areas where sheep or deer are present. The main danger is their ability to pass lyme disease to both dogs and humans. Lyme disease is prevalent in some areas of the USA (see page 164). It remains rare in the UK but its incidence is increasing so it is wise to be aware of it.

The treatment you give your dog for fleas generally works for ticks, but you should discuss the best product to use with your vet.

How to remove a tick

If you spot a tick on your dog, do not try to pluck it off as you risk leaving the hard mouth parts embedded in his skin. The best way to remove a tick is to use a fine pair of tweezers or you can buy a tick remover. Grasp the tick head firmly and then pull the tick straight out from the skin. If you are using a tick remover, check the instructions, as some recommend a circular twist when pulling. When you have removed the tick, clean the area with mild soap and water.

Ear mites

These parasites live in the outer ear canal. The signs of infestation are a brown, waxy discharge, and your dog will continually shake his head and scratch his ear. If you suspect your Cocker has ear mites, a visit to the vet will be needed so that medicated ear drops can be prescribed.

Fur mites

These small, white parasites are visible to the naked eye and are often referred to as 'walking dandruff'. They cause a scurfy coat and mild itchiness. However, they are zoonotic – transferable to humans – so prompt treatment with an insecticide prescribed by your vet is essential.

Harvest mites

These are picked up from the undergrowth, and can be seen as a bright orange patch on the webbing between the toes, although this can also be found elsewhere on the body, such as on the ear flaps. Treatment is effective with the appropriate insecticide.

Skin mites

There are two types of parasite that burrow into a dog's skin. *Demodex canis* is transferred from a mother to her pups while they are feeding. Treatment is with a topical preparation, and sometimes antibiotics are needed.

The other skin mite is *sarcoptes scabiei,* which causes intense itching and hair loss. It is highly contagious, so all dogs in a household will need to be treated, which involves repeated bathing with a medicated shampoo.

Common ailments.

As with all living animals, dogs can be affected by a variety of ailments, most of which can be treated effectively after consulting with your vet, who will prescribe appropriate medication and will advise you on how to care for your dog's needs.

Here are some of the more common problems that could affect your Cocker Spaniel, with advice on how to deal with them.

Anal glands

These are two small sacs on either side of the anus, which produce a dark-brown secretion that dogs use when they mark their territory. The anal glands should empty every time a dog defecates but, if they become blocked or impacted, a dog will experience increasing discomfort. He may nibble at his rear end, or 'scoot' his bottom along the ground to relieve the irritation.

Treatment involves a trip to the vet where the vet will empty the glands manually. It is important to do this without delay or infection may occur.

Dental problems

Good dental hygiene will do much to minimise problems with gum infection and tooth decay. If tartar accumulates to the extent that you cannot remove it by brushing, the vet will need to intervene. In a situation such as this, an anesthetic will need to be administered so the tartar can be removed manually.

Diarrhoea

There are many reasons why a dog has diarrhoea, but most commonly it is the result of scavenging, a sudden change of diet, or an adverse reaction to a particular type of food. The Cocker, with his love for investigating the undergrowth, may well discover something he thinks is appetizing, and so digestive upset caused by scavenging is not unusual.

If your dog is suffering from diarrhoea, the first step is to withdraw food for a day. It is important that he does not dehydrate, so make sure that fresh drinking water is available. However, drinking too much can increase the diarrhoea, which may be accompanied with vomiting, so limit how much he drinks at any one time.

After allowing the stomach to rest, feed a bland diet, such as white fish or chicken with boiled rice, for a few days. In most cases, your dog's motions will return to normal and you can resume your usual feeding, although this should be done gradually.

However, if this fails to work and the diarrhoea persists for more than a few days, you should consult you vet. Your dog may have an infection, which needs to be treated with antibiotics, or the diarrhoea may indicate some other problem which needs expert diagnosis.

Ear infections

The Cocker Spaniel's long ears lying close to the head are a feature of the breed, particularly those bred from show lines. With these type of ears, air cannot circulate as freely as it would in a dog with semi-pricked or pricked ears, so it is important to keep a close check on your Cocker's ears.

A healthy ear is clean with no sign of redness or inflammation, and no evidence of a waxy brown discharge or a foul odor. If you see your dog scratching his ear, shaking his head, or holding one ear at an odd angle, you will need to consult your vet.

The most likely causes are ear mites (see page 172), an infection, or there may a foreign body, such as a grass seed, trapped in the ear.

Depending on the cause, treatment is with medicated ear drops, possibly containing antibiotics. If a foreign body is suspected, the vet will need to carry our further investigations.

Eye problems

Bred as a working dog, it is important that the Cocker's eyes are not large or prominent as they would be vulnerable to injury.

However, if your dog's eyes look red and sore, he may be suffering from Conjunctivitis. This may, or may not be accompanied with a watery or a crusty discharge. Conjunctivitis can be caused by a bacterial or viral infection, it could be the result of an injury, or it could be an adverse reaction to pollen.

You will need to consult your vet for a correct diagnosis, but in the case of an infection, treatment with medicated eye drops is effective. Conjunctivitis may also be the first sign of more serious inherited eye problems (see page 184).

Foreign bodies

In the home, puppies – and some older dogs – cannot resist chewing anything that looks interesting. This is most particularly true of the Cocker – he will always be checking for anything that may be edible.

The toys you choose for your dog should be suitably robust to withstand damage, but children's toys can be irresistible. Some dogs will chew – and swallow – anything from socks, tights, and other items from the laundry basket, to golf balls and stones from the garden. Obviously, these items are indigestible and could cause an obstruction in your dog's intestine, which is potentially lethal.

The signs to look for are vomiting, and a tucked up posture. The dog will often be restless and will look as though he is in pain. In this situation, you must get your dog to the vet without delay as surgery will be needed to remove the obstruction.

The other type of foreign body that may cause problems is grass seed. A grass seed can enter an orifice such as a nostril, down an ear, the gap between the eye and the eyelid, or penetrate the soft skin between the toes. It can also be swallowed.

The introduction of a foreign body induces a variety of symptoms, depending on the point of entry and where it travels to. The signs to look for include head shaking/ear scratching, the eruption of an abscess, sore, inflamed eyes, or a persistent cough. The vet will be able to make a proper diagnosis, and surgery may be required.

Heatstroke

The Cocker is a hardy breed but care should be taken on hot days as heatstroke is a potential danger. When the temperature rises, make sure your dog always has access to shady areas, and wait for a cooler part of the day before going for a walk. Be extra careful if you leave your Cocker in the car, as the temperature can rise dramatically – even on a cloudy day. Heatstroke can happen very rapidly, and unless you are able lower your dog's temperature, it can be fatal.

If your Cocker appears to be suffering from heatstroke, lie him flat and try to reduce his core body temperature by wrapping him in cool towels. A dog should not be immersed in cold water as this will cause the blood vessels to constrict, impeding heat dissipation. As soon as he made some recovery, take him to the vet, where cold intravenous fluids can be administered.

Lameness/limping

There are a wide variety of reasons why a dog can go lame, from a simple muscle strain to a fracture, ligament damage, or more complex problems with the joints which may be an inherited disorder (see page 187). It takes an expert to make a correct diagnosis, so if you are concerned about your dog, do not delay in seeking help.

As your Cocker becomes elderly, he may suffer from arthritis, which you will see as general stiffness, particularly when he gets up after resting. It will help if you ensure his bed is in a warm, draft-free location, and, if your Cocker gets wet after exercise, you must dry him thoroughly.

If your elderly Cocker seems to be in pain, consult your vet who will be able to help with pain relief medication.

Skin problems

If your dog is scratching or nibbling at his skin, the first thing to check for is fleas (see page 170).There are other external parasites which cause itching and hair loss, but you will need a vet to help you find the culprit.

An allergic reaction is another major cause of skin problems. It can be quite an undertaking to find the cause of the allergy, and you will need to follow your vet's advice, which often requires eliminating specific ingredients from the diet, as well as looking at environmental factors.

Inherited disorders

The Cocker Spaniel does have a few breed related disorders, and if a Cocker is diagnosed with any of the diseases listed below, it is important to remember that they can affect offspring, so breeding from affected dogs should be strongly discouraged.

There are now recognised screening tests to enable breeders to check for affected individuals and hence reduce the prevalence of these diseases within the breed.

DNA testing is also becoming more widely available, and as research into the different genetic diseases progresses, more DNA tests are being developed.

Eye disorders

Cockers can be affected by a number of eye disorders. In most cases, testing is carried out by the Canine Eye Registration Foundation in the US; in the

UK there is a combined scheme run by the British Veterinary Association, the Kennel Club and the International Sheep Dog Society.

Generalised Progressive Retinal Atrophy (Gpra)

GPRA is a bilateral degenerative disease of the retina leading initially to night blindness and progressing to complete loss of vision. There may be some association with cataract formation. Clinical identification is by examination of the eye, and the eye tests aim to identify affected individuals.

There is also a DNA test available for the most commonly seen form of GPRA in Cockers, known as prcd_PRA. A simple blood sample or cheek swab can be tested to determine whether a dog is Normal (Clear), a Carrier of the condition or Affected. Carrier dogs will never develop the disease but can produce affected dogs if mated to other carriers. The DNA test means that breeders can identify carriers before breeding and so can now avoid breeding affected dogs.

Retinal Pigment Epithelial Dsytrophy (Rped)

RPED, previously called Centralised Progressive Retinal Atrophy (CPRA), is where an accumulation of pigment occurs in the retina resulting in a slowly progressive loss of vision. There may be some link between RPED and vitamin E deficiency, and supplementation may prove helpful in preventing progression of the disease. Again, eye testing is needed to diagnose the condition.

Goniodysgenesis/primary glaucoma

This is where there is abnormal development of the eye so that fluid that is constantly being produced within the eye (aqueous humour) cannot drain adequately. Over time this results in an increase in pressure within the eye and clinical signs of acute redness and pain. Medication alone is not usually enough and surgery is often needed to relieve the pressure.

Hip dysplasia

This is where the ball and socket joint of the hip develops incorrectly so that the head of the femur (ball) and the acetabulum of the pelvis (socket) do not fit snugly. This results in joint pain and may cause lameness in dogs as young as five months with deterioration into severe arthritis over time.

Cocker Spaniels, like many other breeds, can be affected with HD, and all potential breeding stock should therefore be screened by having their hips scored. In the US, hip scoring is carried out by the Orthopaedic Foundation for Animals. X-rays are submitted when a dog is two years old, categorised as Normal (Excellent, Good, Fair), Borderline, and Dysplastic (Mild, Moderate, Severe). The hip grades of Excellent, Good and Fair are within normal limits and are given OFA numbers.

In the UK, the minimum age for the hips to be assessed by X-ray is 12 months. Each hip can score from a possible perfect 0 to a deformed 53. Both left and right scores are added together to give the total hip score.

Careful and responsible breeding over the years has reduced the prevalence of this disease in Cocker

Spaniels, but care must be taken to ensure that this continues.

Immune mediated hemolytic anaemia

This is a condition where the body's immune system sees the red blood cells in the bloodstream as foreign and destroys them. Cocker Spaniels appear to have a predisposition to this disease.

Presentation of clinical signs can vary from mild to severe anaemia with chronic to acute onset and life threatening collapse due to reduced oxygen carrying capacity of the blood. Often this may be managed medically with immuno-suppressive medications but, if severe, repeated blood transfusions may be necessary.

Familial nephropathy

This disease affects Cocker Spaniels from the age of six months to two years. It is believed to be damage to the glomerular basement membrane in the kidney which causes fatal renal failure. It used to be more prevalent, but breeding schemes have reduced the incidence dramatically, and nowadays it is rarely seen.

A DNA test is also now available, meaning carriers of this condition can be identified prior to breeding. As with prcd_PRA, FN Carriers will never develop the disease but can produce affected dogs if mated to other carriers. The DNA test means that breeders can identify carriers before breeding and so can now avoid breeding affected dogs.

Summing up

It may give the pet owner cause for concern to find about health problems that may affect their dog. But it is important to bear in mind that acquiring some basic knowledge is an asset, as it will allow you to spot signs of trouble at an early stage. Early diagnosis is very often the means to the most effective treatment.

Fortunately, the Cocker Spaniel is a generally healthy and disease-free dog with his only visits to the vet being annual check-ups. In most cases, owners can look forward to enjoying many happy years with this loyal companion.

Useful addresses

Breed & Kennel Clubs
Please contact your Kennel Club to obtain contact information about breed clubs in your area.

UK
The Kennel Club (UK)
1 Clarges Street London, W1J 8AB
Telephone: 0870 606 6750
Fax: 0207 518 1058
Web: www.thekennelclub.org.uk

USA
American Kennel Club (AKC)
5580 Centerview Drive, Raleigh, NC 27606.
Telephone: 919 233 9767
Fax: 919 233 3627
Email: info@akc.org
Web: www.akc.org

United Kennel Club (UKC)
100 E Kilgore Rd, Kalamazoo,
MI 49002-5584, USA.
Tel: 269 343 9020
Fax: 269 343 7037
Web:www.ukcdogs.com

Australia
Australian National Kennel Council (ANKC)
The Australian National Kennel Council is the administrative body for pure breed canine affairs in Australia. It does not, however, deal directly with dog exhibitors, breeders or judges. For information pertaining to breeders, clubs or shows, please contact the relevant State or Territory Body.

International
Fédération Cynologique Internationalé (FCI)
Place Albert 1er, 13, B-6530 Thuin, Belgium.
Tel: +32 71 59.12.38
Fax: +32 71 59.22.29
Web: www.fci.be

Training and behavior
UK
Association of Pet Dog Trainers
Telephone: 01285 810811
Web: www.apdt.co.uk

Canine Behaviour
Association of Pet Behaviour Counsellors
Telephone: 01386 751151
Web: www.apbc.org.uk

USA
Association of Pet Dog Trainers
Tel: 1 800 738 3647
Web: www.apdt.com

American College of Veterinary Behaviorists
Web: www.dacvb.org

American Veterinary Society of Animal Behavior
Web: www.avsabonline.org

Australia
APDT Australia Inc
Web: www.apdt.com.au

For details of regional behaviorists, contact the relevant State or Territory Controlling Body.

Activities
UK
Agility Club
www.agilityclub.co.uk

British Flyball Association
Telephone: 01628 829623
Web: www.flyball.org.uk

USA
North American Dog Agility Council
Web: www.nadac.com

North American Flyball Association, Inc.
Tel/Fax: 800 318 6312
Web: www.flyball.org

Australia
Agility Dog Association of Australia
Tel: 0423 138 914
Web: www.adaa.com.au

NADAC Australia
Web: www.nadacaustralia.com

Australian Flyball Association
Tel: 0407 337 939
Web: www.flyball.org.au

International
World Canine Freestyle Organisation
Tel: (718) 332-8336
Web: www.worldcaninefreestyle.org

Health
UK
British Small Animal Veterinary Association
Tel: 01452 726700
Web: www.bsava.com

Royal College of Veterinary Surgeons
Tel: 0207 222 2001
Web: www.rcvs.org.uk

www.dogbooksonline.co.uk/healthcare

Alternative Veterinary Medicine Centre
Tel: 01367 710324
Web: www.alternativevet.org

USA
American Veterinary Medical Association
Tel: 800 248 2862
Web: www.avma.org

American College of Veterinary Surgeons
Tel: 301 916 0200
Toll Free: 877 217 2287
Web: www.acvs.org

Canine Eye Registration Foundation
The Veterinary Medical DataBases
1717 Philo Rd, PO Box 3007,
Urbana, IL 61803-3007
Tel: 217-693-4800
Fax: 217-693-4801
Web: www.vmdb.org/cerf.html

Orthopaedic Foundation of Animals
2300 E Nifong Boulevard
Columbia, Missouri, 65201-3806
Tel: 573 442-0418
Fax: 573 875-5073
Web: www.offa.org

American Holistic Veterinary Medical
Association
Tel: 410 569 0795
Web: www.ahvma.org

Australia
Australian Small Animal Veterinary
Association
Tel: 02 9431 5090
Web: www.asava.com.au

Australian Veterinary Association
Tel: 02 9431 5000
Web: www.ava.com.au

Australian College Veterinary Scientists
Tel: 07 3423 2016
Web: www.acvsc.org.au

Australian Holistic Vets
Web: www.ahv.com.au